Turn Your
GOD-GIVEN DREAMS INTO REALITY

RICK RENNER

Tulsa, OK

Unless otherwise indicated, all Scripture quotations are taken from the *King James Version* of the Bible.

Scripture quotations marked (*NIV*) are taken from the *Holy Bible: New International Version*®. NIV®. Copyright © 1973, 1978, 1984 by International Bible Society. Used by permission of Zondervan Publishing House. All rights reserved.

Scripture quotations marked *NKJV* are taken from the *New King James Version*®. Copyright © 1982 by Thomas Nelson. Used by permission. All rights reserved.

Scripture quotations marked *AMPC* are taken from *The Amplified Bible. Old Testament* copyright © 1965, 1987 by Zondervan Corporation, Grand Rapids, Michigan. *New Testament* copyright © 1958, 1987 by The Lockman Foundation, La Habra, California. All rights reserved.

Turn Your God-Given Dreams Into Reality
ISBN 978-168031-172-3
Copyright © 2017 by Rick Renner
8316 E. 73rd St.
Tulsa, OK 74133

Published by Harrison House Publishers
Tulsa, OK 74145
www.harrisonhouse.com

2017 New Edition

Editorial Consultant: Cynthia D. Hansen
Text Design: Lisa Simpson, www.SimpsonProductions.net
Cover Design: Debbie Pullman, Zoe Life Creative Media,
www.ZoeLifeCreative.com

Printed in the United States of America.

Delight yourself also in the Lord,
and He shall give you the desires
of your heart.
Commit your way to the Lord,
trust also in Him,
and He shall bring it to pass.
— PSALM 37:4,5 NKJV

Contents

1

⌘

GOD WANTS TO GIVE YOU THE DESIRES OF YOUR HEART

What are the secret dreams in your heart? What does your heart secretly yearn for or hunger after? Is there anything your heart aches to be or to achieve that you have yet to tell anyone about?

When your head hits the pillow every night, what are the thoughts and desires that fill your mind? What secret dreams do you think about when everything gets quiet and you are alone?

Could it be that those dreams you've dismissed as being silly aren't fantasies at all, but a divine plan for your life? Is it possible that *God* put those thoughts deep inside your spirit and soul — thoughts that are now trying to surface in your imagination?

Is God's plan on the inside of you starting to wake up?

Maybe it's time to allow yourself to explore the supernatural possibilities of what you could become and what you could accomplish in life. Perhaps it's God's timing for you to dare to dream — to take the lid off your deepest yearnings.

So as you read this book, I want you to let your imagination become a picture screen. Allow the Holy Spirit to show you the wonder of all God wants you to become!

Satan's Strategy To Deceive

You see, God *wants* to give you the desires, yearnings, and longings of your heart. Psalm 37:4 tells you how He can do it: "Delight thyself also in the Lord; and he shall give thee the desires of thine heart." As long as you delight in the Lord, it is His pleasure to give you the desires that are embedded deep down inside your heart.

I already know what you're asking yourself: *But how can I know whether my dreams are really from God or just my selfish desires?*

The devil is extremely smart in the way he attacks your mind. He knows exactly when to get religious. He knows which questions to ask to make you doubt that God will ever use you. The enemy knows precisely how to keep you stuck right where you are so you'll never be an achiever and an overcomer.

To this end, the devil will ask you deceptive questions, such as:

- *Do you want to succeed because you're selfish?*

- *How do you know you're capable of dealing with success?*

- *Are you one of those people who can't handle the responsibilities that come with success?*

- *Don't you think it's a little arrogant to imagine that God could use you in such a great way?*

- *Is it possible that it's your pride telling you to believe you're supposed to fulfill some great purpose in life?*

Unfortunately, many people easily fall prey to these kinds of lying insinuations because they come from religious backgrounds that never taught them to dream. This deficiency is reinforced by wrong denominational teaching that conditions them to view themselves as lowly "worms" in the eyes of God. As a result, these people accept a low-level existence as their inevitable lot in life.

Regardless of your spiritual background, the devil knows exactly which buttons to push in your emotions to keep you all bound up and depressed. He even knows how to disguise his voice to make you think *God* is talking to you. He wants to get you off track so you will dispel your deepest dreams, casting them off as pure imagination. You see, friend, the devil wants to talk you into settling for a life that is *routine, monotonous, boring,* and *unfulfilling*.

The Devil Has a Plan for Your Life

Jesus taught that the devil comes to us with only three purposes in mind: to steal, to kill, and to destroy.

**The thief cometh not, but for to steal,
and to kill, and to destroy: I am come
that they might have life, and that they
might have it more abundantly.**

—John 10:10

Satan has a plan for you: He wants to kill, steal, and destroy everything in your life. He is after your job, your joy, your happiness, your health, your finances, your marriage, and your kids. The devil wants to ruin anything he can get his hands on — including your dreams!

If Satan can steal the dream God put in your heart, he knows he will obliterate your whole purpose in life. That's why he wants to talk you into throwing your secret dream away. You see, the devil is a dream thief. By stealing your dream, he kills your destiny and destroys your hope of doing or becoming anything significant in life.

(I recommend you read my book *Dream Thieves*. This book is written out of my personal experiences about how to fight the forces in life that come to steal the dream God put in your heart. If you're seeking God's will for your life and you want to know how to keep the devil out of your efforts, this life-changing book is a *must*. Thousands have read it and have been blessed by it.)

So just tell the devil to shut up and stop dropping those religious, nonsensical thoughts into your head. Tell him to hit the road! Let him know you're not going to bite the bait anymore, so he may as well go fishing somewhere else. You're not a sucker anymore! You have just been informed that a deadly hook is hidden inside the bait. That hook is intended to catch hold of you, pull you into the devil's net, and make you a meal for the devil to "chew on" for a long time. But it's not going to hook *you* anymore!

There's no doubt about it!

- The devil wants you to be defeated.

- The devil wants you to struggle throughout your life.

- The devil wants you to be sick, depressed,
  discouraged, and miserable.

- The devil wants you to feel like you
  never "hit the target" with your life.

The enemy wants to make your life nothing
more than a less-than-gratifying, unhappy,
uneventful life — a life that no one even notices
is gone once it is over. That's the devil's plan, and
that's why he has tried so hard to convince you
to settle for the lowest and the least in life.

But the devil doesn't get the final say-so in
the matter! *You* decide the outcome of your life
on this earth!

- It's time for you to get up and get
  moving!

- It's time for you to shove those destructive lies out of your life!

- It's time for you to reach up and grab hold of God's plan for you!

- It's time to let your dreams soar!

- It's time to let the Holy Spirit reveal your purpose in this world!

- It's time for you to realize God has something great and glorious for you to do and to become!

Believe me, friend, God didn't just bring you into the world to take up space and eat food that others could be eating. God has a glorious and wonderful plan for your life, or you wouldn't be here. He has a specific purpose for you to fulfill that is significant in the furtherance of His great plan for mankind.

That's why God wants you to discover the secret dreams and desires of your heart. He is eagerly awaiting the opportunity to manifest those desires to you as you fulfill your divine purpose in life!

2

God's FIRST WORDS

Just for a moment, think back to the creation of man. I want you to see what kind of dream God originally had for mankind — a divine dream that includes YOU.

The FIRST WORDS God spoke to man are recorded in Genesis 1:26: "And God said, Let us make man in our image, after our likeness: and let them have dominion...." Those FIRST WORDS revealed God's original design for man. A few verses later, God continued by saying, "...Be *fruitful*, and *multiply*, and *replenish* the earth, and *subdue* it: and *have dominion*..." (v. 28).

It is obvious that God had good plans in mind when He made man. He wanted man to be *fruitful,* to *multiply,* to *increase.* He wanted man to be in charge — a ruler exercising dominion and great authority over his environment.

Our Embedded Urge To Achieve

Once the world was created, Adam and Eve were at the center of it as *rulers* of a new world. This verse says they were made in God's *likeness.* That means they were supposed to be *like* God.

- God was a *Ruler* — so man was to rule.

- God was a *King* — so man was to be a king.

- God was *all-powerful* — so man was to be powerful.

- God was a *Subduer* — so man was to be a subduer.

God *never* intended for man to be defeated or subdued. In fact, man wasn't defeated or subdued until he *sinned*. That was the moment Satan found a loophole through which he could enter Adam's world and flood it with death, destruction, and defeat (*see* Romans 5:12).

When sin came, God's likeness in man's soul was disfigured. Losing the glory God had created them to live in, Adam and Eve became slaves to the flesh and to the world around them. But centuries later, the death and resurrection of Jesus Christ reversed the perverted, twisted curse Satan had put on man (*see* Romans 5:12-21).

Those FIRST WORDS of God are still deeply embedded inside man's soul. That's why man keeps reaching upward to achieve higher and greater goals.

The urge to achieve is in your bloodstream. It's in your genetic makeup. It's alive and breathing in every single cell of your body.

That insatiable craving to accomplish high goals and to become something significant has been a part of man's makeup ever since God infused it into the bloodstream and genes of mankind's great-grandparents, Adam and Eve. Although the devil has tried to eradicate that craving, it has never been totally expunged from the human soul.

That is why your mind imagines who you could be, what you could achieve, and the impact you could make in this world. God put that dream inside you, so don't let the devil steal it from you. Instead, focus on renewing your mind with the Word of God; then the Holy Spirit can more accurately reveal the *exact plan* God has for you.

The Reason You May Feel Depressed and Defeated

I can tell you why people often feel depressed and defeated about their lives. They were created to be so much, yet they live their lives on such a low level. Therefore, they are miserable and feel as if they are going nowhere with their lives. They are living so far below the FIRST WORDS God ever spoke to man that their souls have become sullen and sad. Something inside them knows they were born to be and to do so much more than what they're experiencing in their low-level existence.

That's why you shouldn't settle for anything less than God's best for your life! He has an awesome plan designed specifically for you. As you renew your mind with His Word and become more in tune to your spirit within, the Holy Spirit will *quicken* that secret dream from way down deep inside you.

Just like a reservoir of oil lying deep below the surface of the earth, waiting to be tapped, those divine plans lie deep within your spirit. And when you finally tap into them, you'll feel like you've hit a *gusher* — a spiritual gusher that brings joy, fulfillment, contentment, and satisfaction to your life!

So let me ask you again:

- Do you have *secret dreams* about yourself?

- Do you privately dream of what you can become?

- Do you ever spend time thinking of ways you can be a blessing to people?

Those secret dreams are God's plans for your life, surfacing from deep within your spirit. Dare to let those dreams develop and materialize on the picture screen of your mind. This may be the beginning of a new and glorious adventure in your life — *the very one God has been waiting for you to step into for a long time.*

3

GOD HAS BEEN WAITING
A LONG TIME
FOR THIS MOMENT!

Before you were ever conceived, God was already designing a master plan for your life. He watched and dreamed of your arrival as you were being formed in your mother's womb. He had many thoughts about His great plans for you — about all you could do and become in life (see Psalm 139:1-17).

It may have taken a little while for you to wake up to what God has had in mind for you, *but the important thing is that you are finally waking up!*

You may ask, "If God deposited His plan for my life into my heart, why don't I know it?"

When your mind is cleaned up and renewed to think like God, it makes it easier for your head to connect with your spirit. This, then, makes it easier for you to perceive God's plan for your life. That is why the Bible commands you to *renew* your mind with the Word of God (*see* Romans 12:2; Ephesians 4:23).

You see, God's Word works like water. It runs over the nooks and crannies of your mind, loosening the dirt and filth of carnal, twisted thinking. Then it carries that garbage out of your thought processes and leaves you with a *renewed mind*.

A renewed mind is one that is free from the defects and the limitations that sin enforces upon our minds. This process is referred to in Ephesians 5:26 as "...the washing of water by the word."

When your mind is washed and renewed by the Word, your mind and spirit begin to work together. Soon your mind *connects* with your spirit, triggering a *divine release* of information inside your spirit that then floods your mind and causes you to perceive your God-ordained destiny. That release is referred to as *revelation.* Once your mind becomes enlightened with this revelation of the plan God designed for your life, you are headed down the road to *success* and *fulfillment* in life.

How To Get Started

I've noticed that even when people *do* know what they are supposed to do in life, they often don't know how to get started. Others want to be used by God, but they become frustrated because their dream doesn't come to pass as quickly or as easily as they had hoped. These people have a real dream from God, but they've been unable to take it from the *dream realm* to the *real realm.* As a result, they feel like failures and often end up believing that God has let them down.

I understand this frustration. When I was a young man just getting started in life, I dreamed big dreams all the time, none of which came true overnight. Some people even called me a *dreamer.* They said I lived in another world — and they were right! I was dreaming and seeing *by faith* what I believed God wanted me to be.

Today I am standing in the reality of the dreams I started nurturing in my heart so many years ago. You can stand in the reality of your secret dreams as well. In the following chapters, I want to show you how to do just that as we talk about moving your dream from the *dream realm* to the *real realm.*

4

✌

My Secret Dream
Seemed Far-Fetched

When I was a teenager, I lay in my bed night after night and dreamed about my future and how God would use me. I knew God had called me to preach, so by faith I would imagine myself preaching the Word of God to masses of people. I yearned for this dream to become a reality.

As a college student, I worked a part-time janitorial job one summer to earn money for my college education. One morning the Spirit of God spoke to me while I was driving my car to work. It was so clear that it almost sounded audible.

He said, *"Rick, I'm going to use your voice to push demonic principalities and powers out of the airwaves. I'm going to use your voice to cleanse the airwaves of evil powers so the Gospel can go into the hearts of men and women in dark regions around the world."*

I was stunned by what God said to me. I was just driving my car, not expecting to hear His voice that day. But I knew God had said something *important* to me. In the years that followed, I never forgot the words I heard that early morning.

I had never previously thought about how the devil used his air-based control center to affect the world's airwaves, although I knew the Bible called Satan "the prince of the power of the air" (Ephesians 2:2). But as I thought about it, I could see exactly what the Lord meant.

The devil has used the technology of radio and television to influence the world with evil images and wrong messages. He has flooded the airwaves with destructive images. God was telling me that He was going to use *my voice* to assist in pushing those powers out of the way so the Gospel could shine into the hearts of men and women in dark regions of the world.

That early morning a *secret dream* was birthed in my heart. I knew the Holy Spirit's words to me meant a television ministry was in my future, but I never told anyone about my secret dream. I was just a young teenager. I didn't want to announce such a grandiose dream to others; it would only make people ridicule me. After all, I knew the story of Joseph and what happened to him when he announced his dream to his brothers!

As I drove to work every morning and back home every night, I began to meditate on what God had told me. Soon I could *see* myself preaching on television. I could *imagine* the sound of my voice traveling across the airwaves of the atmosphere and smashing into evil principalities and powers. I could *visualize* the anointed Word of God shoving those demonic influences out of the way so the Gospel's glorious light could shine into the homes of people who were held captive by Satan's power.

My Dream Was a Seed

At the time, I was just an 18-year-old college student who didn't have a lot of money. I didn't have a clue how God's plan for my life would ever get started. How was I going to get from where I was to the place where my secret dream would become a manifested reality?

Maybe you think *your* dream is far-fetched and unattainable. Don't let that bother you too much. Most God-given dreams are impossible to fulfill in your own natural strength or ability.

Without God's assistance, His vision for your life *is* far-fetched. But Jesus said, "...All things are possible to him that believeth" (Mark 9:23). This means if you have God on your side, you can do *anything* God tells you to do!

The Bible is filled with examples of people who had dreams. Because they refused to give up, they achieved supernatural realities during their lives. Hebrews 11:33,34 tells us that these men and women of God "...through faith subdued kingdoms, wrought righteousness, obtained promises, stopped the mouths of lions, quenched the violence of fire, escaped the edge of the sword, out of weakness were made strong, waxed valiant in fight, turned to flight the armies of the aliens."

It took a lot of hard work, time, and patience, but these biblical dreamers achieved the impossible and experienced what others only fantasize about. Why? Because they were willing to believe that *God* had birthed their

far-fetched dreams in their hearts and that with
His help, they could actually do what He had
called them to do!

Your Dreams Are Like Seeds

By looking at a tiny apple seed, one would
never imagine that thousands and thousands
of apples lie hidden within. All that incredible
potential is locked up *inside* that tiny seed.
To the natural eye, the seed looks small and
insignificant, but God knows its potential. He
also knows that its potential will lie dormant
until someone nurtures it, fertilizes it, and
helps it grow.

Some seeds occasionally fall to the ground
and accidentally take root. But this isn't the
way it normally happens. *Accidental fruit-
producers are pretty rare.* Most fruit-yielding
trees come from seeds that were planted and
nurtured with tender care. Yes, there are wild

trees that produce fruit. But because they were not nurtured properly, they usually don't wear as well nor produce as much as cultivated fruit trees.

Dreams are like seeds — they need to be nurtured and fertilized. That time of nurturing may take awhile, but eventually the tiny seeds of vision God has sown in your heart will begin to grow and produce fruit. It just takes time, effort, and patience.

I want to help you build a foundation for fruitfulness in your life. You see, there are things you can do to cultivate those "dream seeds" until you reach your God-given potential. Rather than sit around and just "hope" your dream will someday come to pass, you can learn how to develop and prepare yourself for the day that dream springs up in your life and makes *you* a fruit-producer.

Don't wait until later to get started. If you're called and have a vision from God, you need to get started *right now*. Don't deceive yourself by waiting for that "golden moment" when you get your big break and success comes to you with no effort. That's not a dream from God — that's a hallucination!

It took me some time, but I learned how to move the far-fetched dream God gave me as a teenager from the *dream realm* to the *real realm*. If you want to do the same, I encourage you to get on the road to your destiny today. *Keep reading, and you'll understand what I mean!*

5

∽

Moving From the *Dream Realm* to the *Real Realm*

There is a cost involved in the fulfillment of all dreams and visions. Whether it's a ministry dream or a business dream, it's going to require a lot of hard work and patience to move that vision from the dream realm to the real realm.

Let's use the example of the apostle Paul. God's plan for Paul's life was huge. It was a plan that would take him to the farthest ends of his world. It would guide him through difficult and dangerous places. But it took more than

wishful thinking for Paul to fulfill the vision
God gave him. It required a lot of patience,
hard work, and endurance.

(I want to encourage you to read Paul's
incredible story in my book *Say Yes!* On pages
58-93, I explain all the seemingly impossible
obstacles Paul faced and overcame as he
pursued God's will for his life.)

That's why you have to make Proverbs
28:19 (*NIV*) the guiding principle for fulfilling
your dreams and desires in life. It says, "Those
who work their land will have abundant food,
but those who chase fantasies will have their fill
of poverty." The principle in this verse promises
that if you work hard, you will enjoy abundance
in your future. God guarantees it!

In Chapter Five of my book, *The Point of No
Return*, I discuss the five primary reasons people
fail in life. Two of those reasons are *laziness* and
unrealistic expectations. People mistakenly expect

that they can just sit around and pray all the time, waiting for success to just drop out of Heaven and take them by surprise.

If that's you, you're in for a rude awakening! You have to put your hand to the plow and do your part to make any dream or desire come to pass.

Paul referred to the "work of the ministry" in his epistles (Ephesians 4:12). Although prayer was a key part of his ministry, he knew it was going to take more than praying to get the job done. For Paul to fulfill the assignment God gave him, it was going to take *work*.

A 'Take-It-Easy' Approach to Life

We live in a world that loves to take it easy. We want instant results — and we want them *right now*. Technology has made almost everything instantly accessible. Our entire Western lifestyle is centered around making things as *easy, fast, effortless,* and *painless* as possible.

The younger generation is so accustomed to getting everything they want that they don't understand there is a price to pay for true success. But whether they like it or not, the fact remains: True greatness, great achievements, and real success won't float to them on clouds that suddenly materialize above their heads. If anyone wants to achieve something great and significant, he or she will have to put a lot of hard work and effort into making it happen.

Let's go back to our example of the apostle Paul. He was a man who achieved incredible feats, so it's important for us to understand:

- How did Paul do it?

- What kind of attitude did he have?

- What did he do to fulfill the assignment God gave to him?

I believe the answers to these questions can be found in an example Paul gave us in the book of First Corinthians.

The Essential Attitude

In First Corinthians 4:1, Paul wrote, "Let a man so account of us, as of the ministers of Christ, and stewards of the mysteries of God."

I want you to especially notice the word "ministers" in this verse. Before you get any religious connotations from this word, let me tell you Paul chose this word because it conveys the essential attitude necessary to get a job done — especially the work of the ministry. However, it doesn't apply only to ministry. It is the *essential attitude* you must possess to take any desire of your heart from the *dream realm* to the *real realm*.

This word "ministers" that Paul used is taken from the Greek word *huperetas*. It was used in classical Greek society to describe *low-class criminals*. Paul chose this strange word because of the images connected with it.

The first time I studied this Greek word, I wondered:

- Why would Paul use such a word to describe ministers?

- Why does he call ministers "criminals"?

- Why would he speak so condescendingly about ministers?

- Why did Paul use this ugly word to describe himself?

- Is he using this word picture to make a point?

After a lot of digging into the original Greek, I found out exactly why Paul used this word. He was a successful man who understood

what it took to get a job done — and no word
more vividly explains this work ethic than the
Greek word *huperetas*. Let me show you what I
mean in the next chapter.

6

∽

TAKE YOUR SEAT
IN THE SHIP

The word *huperetas* in First Corinthians 4:1 described the very lowest class of criminals. These particular people were considered to be the scum of the earth! In fact, these criminals were so low, so detestable, and so contemptible that they were outcast and removed from society, assigned to live the balance of their lives in the bottom galleys of huge shipping vessels. There they literally became the engines of those huge ships.

And the harsh assignment of these *huperetas* wasn't temporary, either. They were sentenced to live the rest of their lives in the darkness below the deck — endlessly rowing, rowing, and rowing. Their entire existence was devoted to keeping that ship moving toward its ultimate destination!

These *huperetas* were officially called "under-rowers" because they lived and rowed down in the bottom of the ship. Day after day, their job was to heave those massive oars forward and backward, pushing them through the water to make the ship move through the sea.

Take Your Place in God's Plan!

This word *huperetas* is the same word the apostle Paul uses to describe those of us who are faithfully trying to do what God has called us to do! According to the Bible, we are the "under-rowers of Christ." This means, above all else, that God has called us to take our place in His plan — to grab hold of an oar, so to speak, and begin to serve Him practically in some way. We are to keep rowing, rowing, rowing, and rowing, doing our part and fulfilling what He has asked us to do.

Some people tend to sit and watch as achievers reach out to do the impossible. But if you are going to join the ranks of those achievers, you'll have to do more than just sit around and talk about it. You'll need to say *yes* to what the Lord is urging you to do.

And remember — those "under-rowers" didn't quickly finish their assignment of rowing; it was their responsibility for a lifetime. In the same way, you need to realize that the secret dream God has put in your heart probably won't be achieved quickly either. It may be an assignment that will last for the rest of your life.

I recommend that you mentally prepare yourself for a long-term stint at doing what God is calling you to do. It will almost certainly take unbelievable strength and energy to move that vision from the realm of dreams to the realm of reality.

So jump into the bottom of the boat, take your place on the "under-rowers' seat," and begin rowing with all your might. With each step of obedience you take and each day of faithfulness you live, your little part will help move the "boat" closer to the desired destination — the ultimate fulfillment of God's plans and purposes in these last days!

Develop a Team Mentality

We can learn more about how to fulfill our secret dreams as we discover more about the *huperetas* of ancient times. Each criminal was placed on a bench. There he was chained to a post, and a huge oar was placed into his hands. On the bench alongside him sat other criminals who were also working hard to keep that ship moving.

These men who were seated on the same bench shared common chains, held a common oar, and worked the same number of hours. They all had to provide equal labor to the task. Their entire lives became a group effort. *They became inseparable from the other men who were on the bench with them.*

Likewise, you'll find that God won't call you to do a big job all by yourself. He will call others at the same time to assist you. When you say *yes* to the will of God — when you jump into the middle of your assigned task and surrender your time, money, talents, and ideas to the Lord — you will discover that others will be right there by your side to help you with the task. *You're not the only one to whom God has been speaking!*

You Cannot Fulfill Your Desires and Dreams Alone

It would have been impossible for one servant to move an entire ship by himself. It required the strength and effort of many servants working together in order to move those huge ships.

In the same way, you cannot accomplish what God has called you to do all alone! *Look around you!* Look at the people God has placed around you to help you fulfill your dream. Don't ignore them, thinking you can do it alone. If your vision from the Lord is big, it will require others to become involved in what you are doing.

I wouldn't be able to fulfill what God has told me to do if I had to do it by myself. The vision is too big and demanding. That's why God didn't stop after He called me. He also called others to stand with me, pray with me, and stay for the long haul, working beside me "on the under-rowers' bench." Their call is just as real as my call. They will answer for their part just as I will answer for mine. And when rewards are given, they will be rewarded for how they helped "row the boat" and keep this ministry moving forward to reach millions of souls.

For example, the Lord has called me to take the teaching of the Bible to spiritually hungry people in the former Soviet Union every day through our media outreach. But at the same time He placed this vision in my heart, He also called partners to pray for the program, pay for television time, and support our ministry in the United States. Without our partners, I couldn't do my part in the former USSR. They are equally as important as Denise and me and our ministry team.

How about the staff members of our television ministry outreach, such as our television producers, editors, and secretaries? Or how about the dedicated workforce who answer thousands of responses each year from people who view our teaching on various media?

Since 1992, this television workforce has answered millions of letters from those who have written to Denise and me as a result of watching our television program. Our media department has also edited thousands of programs on TV alone and distributed nearly 200,000 separate showings to all of the seven time zones of the former Soviet Union — and that doesn't even include our teachings that can be seen on a host of other forms of media.

These staff members are the ones who do the work behind the scenes so that these programs can go into millions of homes every day of the week. I am so thankful for those on my team whom God called to help me with this awesome task, because this job is too big for me to do alone!

Your Partners in Life

Likewise, if you are going to fulfill the dream God has given *you*, you will have to learn how to cooperate with other key people — *your partners in life* — who can assist you in fulfilling that dream.

When rewards were given to one bench of "under-rowers" for their extremely hard work, every man in the group was rewarded. Since they labored at the same task, shared the same oar, and sweated the same amount of sweat, the entire bench of workers was equally rewarded. On the other hand, if one rower on a bench was lazy and kept the whole bench of rowers from carrying their share of the load on the ship, every rower on that bench was punished.

In other words, the difference in one coworker's attitude was so powerful that he had the ability to bring about victory or defeat for his entire team. Since each member was vital to success, the under-rowers' entire existence became a group effort. *Therefore, they had to learn how to function as a team.*

When these men rowed, the boat moved. When they stopped rowing, the boat stopped. These servants were the driving force behind the speed of the ship. If they ever stopped working hard at rowing, the ship stayed motionless in the water. It was totally dependent on the rowers in the bottom of the boat, powerless to travel anywhere without them.

Similarly, if you are going to move ahead with what God has called you to do — *whether it is your ministry, your family, or your business —* you must learn how to be a faithful servant, working together with others as a unified team "in the bottom of the boat."

The bottom of the boat may not be the most pleasurable place to be. Serving day in and day out may seem monotonous and almost boring at times. But sticking with the vision and continuing to row will eventually produce eternal results for the Kingdom of God!

7

✑

DON'T JUMP SHIP!

If you had been allowed to peek into the bottom galley of those huge ships of biblical times, you would have seen that these prisoners were all chained to a post near their respective benches. There was a good reason for this heavy chain.

Because their work was so hard and their destiny was sealed in the bottom of that ship, these men's minds would wander to more beautiful, restful places where palm trees overlooked sandy seashores or where tall pines swayed in refreshing mountain breezes. Had the "under-rowers" not been chained to their post, they may have attempted to escape from their bench to find a more restful lifestyle somewhere else. Therefore, chains kept the men where they belonged — *right in the bottom of the boat, tied to their post with oar in hand, compelled to effectively do their job.*

Likewise, you must know that as you seek to do God's will for your life, you'll have to take on all kinds of assaults and challenges that inevitably accompany obedience. And let me warn you, there will be times when your flesh tries to find a way to "jump ship" and get out from underneath the pressure of obeying God! Your flesh would love to be "led" somewhere else where faith isn't required and the crucifixion of flesh doesn't seem so necessary.

See It Through to the End

You see, it's easy to *start* obeying God. Initiating a project is fun and exciting, and it's always the easiest part. The difficult part is sticking with that project and seeing it through all the way to the end.

The real test comes when the excitement is gone and the reality of hard work and commitment begins to dawn on you. That's always the golden moment when the flesh is tempted to forget you ever heard from God and begins to look for a way out!

If we are not really committed to go all the way in fulfilling our God-assigned task, we probably won't do it. Therefore, you and I must be absolutely committed to do what God has called us to do, "chaining ourselves" to our decision to obey so we cannot flee in hard times.

If God has called you, don't jump ship! He needs you in the bottom of the boat in order to keep the Body of Christ moving forward toward maturity. *You* are very important!

I'm sure there were times when the "under-rowers" said, *"I'm tired of rowing! Get me off this boat!"* They probably had to be reminded, "You are the engines of the ship. If you get off the boat, the boat will stop moving. You are too vital to jump ship now. We can't go on without you!"

Feeling Sorry for Yourself Is a Waste of Time

There were also probably times when these men in the bottom of the ship said, "No one appreciates us or says 'thank you' for what we do! We work, work, work, and *work*, and yet we are treated like slaves! I just wish someone would occasionally show some appreciation."

I make it my aim to always thank people for what they do. When people give to our ministry or write to let me know they are praying for me, I always try to go out of my way to say "thank you" because I know how much it means to feel appreciated.

We all want to be appreciated. I like to be thanked when I work hard, just as we all do. This is a natural, normal desire. If we'd all just treat each other with good manners in the Body of Christ, it would solve a world of problems and remedy a lot of hurt feelings.

But people are people, and sometimes they forget to say "thank you." It's absolutely true that people should be more thoughtful and appreciative. But the bottom line is this: Ultimately, it doesn't matter whether or not those around us ever show us appreciation for what we do. *If the boat is going to move, we must row the boat!*

Just like these "under-rowers" we've been studying, if we stop rowing — if we stop doing our job — it could possibly jeopardize the destiny God has called us to fulfill. If the boat is going to move, we must row, whether or not we ever hear the words "thank you" from anyone.

That is the hard reality of life for all of us as servants of God. Yes, it would be nice to hear "thank you" from time to time. But lack of appreciation must not affect our determination to row our boat and do what God has called us to do.

Can you now see why Paul chose such a word to describe the essential attitude we must have to do the will of God? You must be willing to be a "prisoner" of Jesus Christ, taken captive by Him to do His will for the rest of your life.

When you said *yes* to the will of God, you surrendered to Him, agreeing to pick up the "oar" He has placed before you. For you, that oar may be a ministry God has given you or a position serving in the local church or a certain business. Perhaps God has instructed you to give money regularly to a ministry like ours.

Whatever responsibility God has set before you, it's time for you to grab hold of that "oar." Then, like the "under-rowers" who rowed in order to move those big ships, you must begin a lifelong occupation of "rowing" to advance the cause God has put on your heart.

From now on, your lifelong commitment needs to be *"I REFUSE to jump ship!"*

8

⁂

It's Time for You To Get Started!

Perhaps you are at that stage in your walk with God where you know what He has called you to do, but you don't yet know how to get started. I'm going to make some practical suggestions in this final chapter to help you get headed in the right direction.

As you read these suggestions, you'll see that I believe in the law of sowing and reaping as one of the basic principles of life. Galatians 6:7 teaches that what you *sow*, you will *reap*. If you want to reap glorious results from the dreams God has placed in your heart, you will have to sow some seeds to give birth to those dreams and then nurture them to maturity in your life.

This is why I highly recommend the following: If you don't yet know how to get started on fulfilling *your* dream, you should get involved in helping someone else fulfill *his* dream. What you do for others will come back to you. *That's one aspect of the law of sowing and reaping.*

It is important that you take advantage of this preparation time in your life. Use it as a season to invest in your own future by sowing seeds into someone else's future. Those seeds of being a blessing to someone else will eventually come back to you as a harvest of blessings in your own life, ministry, or business.

Six Suggestions To Get You Headed Toward Your Goal

In order for the plan of God to be fulfilled in your life, you have to do your part to start moving toward your final destination. The following six suggestions are intended to help you to do that. These recommendations provide a way for you to gain momentum in your life so your dream can begin the transition out of the *dream realm* into the *real realm*.

1. **Decide to *start* serving.**

   ➤ It's time to get in or get out. Quit sitting on the fence, watching everyone else contribute. You can make a big difference in someone else's life if you'll just make the decision to be a life-changer!

   ➤ Look around you and assess the various needs you see. Decide which needs you may be able to help meet. Prayerfully determine how your talents, insights, gifts, and money can best touch souls and bring them into the Kingdom of God.

➤ Once you decide to serve, go for it "full throttle"! Actively set your faith on fulfilling the task. Believe for God's blessing to come upon it. Make it a priority in your prayer life, praying and serving as if the entire project depended on you.

2. **Decide *how* you are going to serve.**

➤ Seek guidance from the Lord regarding *how* you are supposed to serve. For instance, are you supposed to get *personally involved* by going to your local church or someone else's ministry and donating your time and labor?

➤ Are you supposed to serve by giving *financially* to the work of the Lord? It takes fuel to run any ship, so your finances provide a powerful means of serving. Giving is one of the most effective ways to help promote and advance the cause of the Gospel.

➤ Is it possible that you are supposed to both personally serve *and* give of your finances?

3. **Decide *where* you are going to serve.**

➤ Don't volunteer for just any ol' thing that comes along. Instead, ask the Holy Spirit to show you *where* you are supposed to serve.

➤ Once the Lord shows you where to serve, go for it with all your heart. Don't be a low-level performer at anything God calls you to do. Give your best to the assigned task and remember that there is a reward awaiting you and your own team in the future.

4. **Decide what *level of commitment* you are willing to make.**

➤ Don't *overcommit* yourself by promising to do something that isn't possible for you to do. Even if your heart wants to say, "Yes, yes, I'll do that," step back and ask, "Is this realistic? Am I going to be able to do what I'm committing to?"

➤ Evaluate how this level of commitment fits in with all the other commitments you've already made. When you commit to do something, people think they can depend on you. So if you back out of your commitment later because it is too much for you to handle, you mess up the plan for everyone else involved. It is better to move more slowly in the beginning so you can make sure you're making the right decision.

➤ Before you make a financial commitment to a church or ministry, make
sure it's a commitment you can really
keep. If your heart is crying out to give
financially, act on that desire.

➤ However, first analyze what amount
you can actually give. If you have the
ability to give large amounts, go for
it! But if you need to start by giving
smaller amounts because your financial
resources are limited, that's all right too.
It's better to commit to an amount that
is actually achievable than to make a
financial commitment that is larger
than your current ability to fulfill.

5. **Decide to make a habit of *sowing seed* —
and start immediately.**

➤ Galatians 6:7 says, "…Whatsoever a
man soweth, that shall he also reap."
This law of sowing and reaping works

for everyone in the world. *What you sow is exactly what you are going to reap.* It may take awhile, but harvest day is coming if you've been planting seeds along the way. So decide to become a sower immediately — *and start sowing those seeds today!*

➤ You also need to decide *what* you are going to sow. Since Galatians 6:7 says, "...Whatsoever a man soweth, *that* shall he also reap," it is very important to know what you want to reap. Determining what you want your harvest to be is the best way to determine what you should sow.

➤ For instance, if you need time, you should be sowing time. If you need love, you should be sowing love. If you need friendship, you should be sowing friendship. If you need money, you should be sowing money. This is a law of God that always works. So look at what you need to reap, and then start sowing your seed accordingly.

➤ You need to decide *where* you are going to start sowing seed. As you make that decision, I urge you to make sure you sow your seed into *good* ground. By that, I mean you should sow seed into a church, ministry, or organization that is truly accomplishing something profitable and good. Don't throw your seed into ground that doesn't produce excellent fruit. Look for fruit-producers. Once you find them, you'll know where you should plant your seed.

➤ I also strongly recommend that you sow your seed into what you want to become. I plant my seeds into ministries I believe in and into ministries from which I want a particular harvest. The

71

Bible promises that we become "par-
takers of the grace" that is upon any
ministry we sow into (Philippians 1:7).

➤ Therefore, I carefully choose where I sow
my seed. I sow into ministries that have
something I desire for myself, because
the grace that is on that ministry is the
grace that will flow back into my life.

6. **Decide that you will not stop for any
reason.**

➤ Galatians 6:9 continues, "And let us
not be weary in well doing: for in due
season we shall reap, if we faint not."
Keep your eyes on the prize, and don't
allow weariness to knock you out of
the game!

➤ The Bible promises that your due
season is coming. Even if it looks like
it's taking longer than you thought

for your harvest to come back to you, hang on tight, and keep doing what you know God wants you to do. Your "due season" is on its way.

➤ Keep your level of expectancy very high. God *promises* your "due season" *will* come if you don't faint and give up. So don't let the devil or discouraging circumstances maneuver you out of the manifestation you've been waiting for. The moment you're on the brink of moving your dream from the *dream realm* to the *real realm* is usually the time the devil tries the hardest to get you to quit!

Your Dream Is About To Become Reality

If you apply these six recommendations to your life, it won't be long until your dream is launched out of the *dream realm* straight into the *real realm*!

These principles of God's Word always work — *in every country, in every culture, and for every person*. If you will follow these principles, they will go to work for *you*. They will bring you the very dream you've been longing to see manifested in your life.

Don't waste any time just sitting around and waiting for something to happen. It's time for you to jump into the bottom of the boat, take your place on that bench next to God's other dreamers and workers, and expend whatever level of energy is necessary to get that ship moving to its final destination.

And if you don't know how to get your own dream moving yet, take this time to sow your time, talent, and money into someone else's dream. Don't worry, thinking that you're wasting your time, talent, and money on someone else. Remember, the law of sowing and reaping is always in operation. *What you do for someone else is exactly what will come back to you!*

Let your dreams take your mind and your faith to places you've never been before. Take the lid off your imagination, and let the Holy Spirit show you who you can be and what you can do.

Jesus said, "...All things are possible to him that believeth" (Mark 9:23). So release your faith, and allow it to carry you into the realm of supernatural possibilities where secret dreams come true!

Scriptures on
God-Given Dreams
for Prayer

Trust in the Lord, and do good; so shalt thou dwell in the land, and verily thou shalt be fed. Delight thyself also in the Lord: and he shall give thee the desires of thine heart. Commit thy way unto the Lord; trust also in him; and he shall bring it to pass (Psalm 37:3-5).

My son, if thou wilt receive my words, and hide my commandments with thee; So that thou incline thine ear unto wisdom, and apply thine heart to understanding.... Then shalt thou understand the fear of the Lord, and find the knowledge of God. For the Lord giveth wisdom: out of his mouth cometh knowledge and understanding. He layeth up sound wisdom for the righteous: he is a buckler to them that walk uprightly. He keepeth the paths of judgment, and preserveth the way of his saints.

Then shalt thou understand righteousness, and judgment, and equity; yea, every good path (Proverbs 2:1,2,5-9).

For I know the thoughts and plans that I have for you, says the Lord, thoughts and plans for welfare and peace and not for evil, to give you hope in your final outcome (Jeremiah 29:11 *AMPC*).

Likewise the Spirit also helps in our weaknesses. For we do not know what we should pray for as we ought, but the Spirit Himself makes intercession for us with groanings which cannot be uttered. Now He who searches the hearts knows what the mind of the Spirit is, because He makes intercession for the saints according to the will of God. And we know that all things work together for good to those who love God, to those who are the called according to His purpose (Romans 8:26-28 *NKJV*).

But as it is written, Eye hath not seen, nor ear heard, neither have entered into the heart of

man, the things which God hath prepared for
them that love him. But God hath revealed
them unto us by his Spirit: for the Spirit sear-
cheth all things, yea, the deep things of God.
For what man knoweth the things of a man,
save the spirit of man which is in him? even
so the things of God knoweth no man, but
the Spirit of God. Now we have received, not
the spirit of the world, but the spirit which is
of God; that we might know the things that
are freely given to us of God (1 Corinthians
1:9-12).

In Him we also were made [God's] heritage
(portion) and we obtained an inheritance;
for we had been foreordained (chosen and
appointed beforehand) in accordance with
His purpose, Who works out everything in
agreement with the counsel and design of His
[own] will (Ephesians 1:11 *AMPC*).

Now to Him Who, by (in consequence of) the
[action of His] power that is at work within
us, is able to [carry out His purpose and] do

superabundantly, far over and above all that we [dare] ask or think [infinitely beyond our highest prayers, desires, thoughts, hopes, or dreams] — to Him be glory in the church and in Christ Jesus throughout all generations forever and ever... (Ephesians 3:20 *AMPC*).

Look carefully then how you walk! Live purposefully and worthily and accurately, not as the unwise and witless, but as wise (sensible, intelligent people), making the very most of the time [buying up each opportunity], because the days are evil. Therefore do not be vague and thoughtless and foolish, but understanding and firmly grasping what the will of the Lord is (Ephesians 5:15-17 *AMPC*).

Therefore do not cast away your confidence, which has great reward. For you have need of endurance, so that after you have done the will of God, you may receive the promise (Hebrews 10:35,36 *NKJV*).

PRAYER OF SALVATION

When Jesus Christ comes into your life, you are immediately emancipated — totally set free from the bondage of sin! If you have never received Jesus as your personal Savior, it is time to experience this new life for yourself. The first step to freedom is simple. Just pray this prayer from your heart:

Lord, I can never adequately thank You for all You did for me on the Cross. I am so undeserving, Jesus, but You came and gave Your life for me anyway.

I repent and turn from my sins right now. I receive You as my Savior, and I ask You to wash away my sin by Your precious blood. I thank You from the depths of my heart for doing what no one else could do for me. Had it not been for

Your willingness to lay down Your life for me, I would be eternally lost.

Thank You, Jesus, that I am now redeemed by Your blood. You bore my sin, my sickness, my pain, my lack of peace, and my suffering on the Cross. Your blood has covered my sin, washed me whiter than snow, and given me rightstanding with the Father. I have no need to be ashamed of my past sins, because I am now a new creature in You. Old things have passed away, and all things have become new because I am in Jesus Christ (1 Corinthians 5:17).

Because of You, Jesus, today I am forgiven; I am filled with peace; and I am a joint heir with You! Satan no longer has a right to lay any claim on me. From a grateful heart, I will faithfully serve You the rest of my days!

If you prayed this prayer from your heart, something amazing has happened to you. No longer a servant to sin, you are now a servant of Almighty God. The evil spirits that once exacted every ounce of your being and required your all-inclusive servitude no longer possess the authorization to control you or to dictate your destiny!

As a result of your decision to turn your life over to Jesus Christ, your eternal home has been decided forever. Heaven is now your permanent address.

God's Spirit has moved into your own human spirit, and you have become the "temple of God" (1 Corinthians 6:19). What a miracle! To think that God, by His Spirit, now lives inside of you!

Now you have a new Lord and Master, and His name is Jesus. From this moment on, the Spirit of God will work in you and supernaturally energize you to fulfill God's will for your life. Everything will change for you now — and it's all going to change for the best!

REFERENCE BOOK LIST

1. *How To Use New Testament Greek Study Aids* by Walter Jerry Clark (Loizeaux Brothers).

2. *Strong's Exhaustive Concordance of the Bible* by James H. Strong.

3. *The Interlinear Greek-English New Testament* by George Ricker Berry (Baker Book House).

4. *The Englishman's Greek Concordance of the New Testament* by George Wigram (Hendrickson).

5. *New Thayer's Greek-English Lexicon of the New Testament* by Joseph Thayer (Hendrickson).

6. *The Expanded Vine's Expository Dictionary of New Testament Words* by W. E. Vine (Bethany).

7. *New International Dictionary of New Testament Theology* (*DNTT*); Colin Brown, editor (Zondervan).

8. *Theological Dictionary of the New Testament* (*TDNT*) by Geoffrey Bromiley; Gephard Kittle, editor (Eerdmans Publishing Co.).

9. *The New Analytical Greek Lexicon*; Wesley Perschbacher, editor (Hendrickson).

10. *The Linguistic Key to the Greek New Testament* by Fritz Rienecker and Cleon Rogers (Zondervan).

11. *Word Studies in the Greek New Testament* by Kenneth Wuest, 4 Volumes (Eerdmans).

12. *New Testament Words* by William Barclay (Westminster Press).

About the Author

Rick Renner is a prolific author and a highly respected Bible teacher and leader in the international Christian community. Rick is the author of more than 30 books, including the bestsellers *Dressed To Kill* and *Sparkling Gems From the Greek 1*, which have sold more than 3 million copies combined.

In 1991, Rick and his family moved to what is now the former Soviet Union. Today he is the senior pastor of the Moscow Good News Church and the founder of a large media outreach that today broadcasts teaching from the Bible to countless Russian-speaking and English-speaking viewers around the world via multiple satellites and the Internet. He is also the founder of Rick Renner Ministries, based in Tulsa, Oklahoma. Rick's wife and lifelong ministry partner, Denise, along with their three sons — Paul, Philip, and Joel — and their families, lead this amazing work with the help of their committed leadership team.

Contact Renner Ministries

For further information
about RENNER Ministries, please contact
the RENNER Ministries office nearest you,
or visit the ministry website at
www.renner.org.

ALL USA
CORRESPONDENCE:
RENNER Ministries
P. O. Box 702040
Tulsa, OK 74170-2040
(918) 496-3213
Or 1-800-RICK-593
Email: renner@renner.org
Website: www.renner.org

MOSCOW OFFICE:
RENNER Ministries
P. O. Box 789
Moscow 101000, Russia
+7 (495) 727-1467
Email: partner@rickrenner.ru
Website: www.rickrenner.ru

RIGA OFFICE:
RENNER Ministries
Unijas 99
Riga LV-1084, Latvia
+(371) 780-2150
Email: info@goodnews.lv

KIEV OFFICE:
RENNER Ministries
P. O. Box 300
Kiev 01001, Ukraine
+38 (044) 451-8315
Email: partner@rickrenner.ru
Website: www.rickrenner.ru

OXFORD OFFICE:
RENNER Ministries
Box 7, 266 Banbury Road
Oxford OX2 7DL, England
+44 (7522) 443955
Email: europe@renner.org

THE HARRISON HOUSE VISION

Proclaiming the truth and the power

of the Gospel of Jesus Christ with excellence.

Challenging Christians

to live victoriously,

grow spiritually,

know God intimately.

Harrison House

For all the latest Harrison House
product information,
including new releases,
email subscriptions,
testimonies, and monthly specials,
please visit **harrisonhouse.com**.